World Faiths

SIKHISM

Joy Barrow

Chrysalis Education

WORLD FAITHS

Buddhism   Christianity
Hinduism   Islam
Judaism   Sikhism

Produced by Bender Richardson White, PO Box 266,
Uxbridge, UB9 5NX

Distributed in the United States by
Smart Apple Media
1980 Lookout Drive, North Mankato, Minnesota 56003

ISBN 1-59389-134-2

The Library of Congress control number 2003105009

Editorial Manager: Joyce Bentley   Senior Editor: Sarah Nunn
Project Editor: Lionel Bender   Text Editor: Michael March, Peter Harrison
Designer: Richard Johnson   Art Editor: Ben White
Proofreader: Jennifer Smart   Production: Kim Richardson
Picture Researchers: Joanne O'Brien at Circa Photo Library, and Cathy Stastny
Cover Make-up: Mike Pilley, Radius   Maps and Charts: Stefan Chabluk

Thanks to Joanne O'Brien at ICOREC, Manchester, for planning the
structure and content of these books.

Printed in Hong Kong
10 9 8 7 6 5 4 3 2 1

Picture Acknowledgments
We wish to thank the following individuals and organizations for their help and assistance, and for
supplying material in their collections: Dr Joy Barrow: pages 1, 5 center, 5 bottom, 8, 14, 16, 17, 24,
26, 27, 29, 30, 45, 46, 48–49. Circa Photo Library: pages 3, 15, 44; (William Holtby) cover; (John
Smith) 5 top, 19, 28, 31, 33, 36, 47, 52–53; (Christine Osborne) 6, 7, 9, 18, 20, 25, 32; (Bipin J. Mistry)
10; (Twin Studio) 11, 12–13, 13, 21 (art by Amrit and Robindra Singh), 22, 50–51. Corbis Images:
(Annie Griffiths Belt) 34; (Robert Holmes) 35; (William Whitehurst) 37; (Chris Lisle) 39; 41; (Earl &
Nazima Kowall) 42. Harmeet Kaur: 4. Bender Richardson White: 23, 54-55. Topham Photo Library:
(Press Association) 38, 43 (UPP) 40.

CONTENTS

Harmeet Kaur's Story

Harmeet Kaur is 23 years old and studying dentistry in London, England. She is a Sikh who aspires to follow the teachings of her faith both in her deeds and in her outward appearance. She lives at home with her parents, grandmother, older brother, and younger sister.

"I COME FROM a religious family. Sikhism has always been the way of life I wanted to follow. When I was 14, I committed myself to it fully and started to attend group discussions about Sikhism led by older teenagers.

When I was 16, I began to wear a *dastar*, or turban, and to follow the daily practice of a committed Sikh. When I was about 18, I made a formal commitment to obey the Sikh way of life at the ceremony called *amrit sanskar*.

Every morning, I get up at about five o'clock, shower, and then recite the Sikhs' five morning prayers. At seven in the morning, I and my parents visit the *gurdwara*. This is where Sikhs meditate on God's name. We spend about half an hour there in prayer.

From nine in the morning till five in the afternoon, I attend university. As I work, I try to repeat God's name in my mind, over and over. That does not mean that I am not concentrating when I am filling someone's teeth. Rather, it is like a child playing with a kite. The child is aware of the kite and makes all the necessary adjustments to keep it in the air, but can still talk to friends at the same time. Repeating God's name in this way should be automatic, but I admit that I have not yet reached that stage.

For just over a year, I have been learning to play the *sarangi*, a traditional Indian stringed instrument. This is so that I can accompany the *kirtan* – songs praising God – which are an important part of a gurdwara service.

Once a month on a Saturday evening, young Sikhs play kirtan at a local gurdwara. I am not yet a skilled enough sarangi player to join in with the musicians, but I do take part in the singing.

Sometimes the young people from my gurdwara organize a get-together at a Sikh camp. There, we can learn more about our religion from other Sikhs and enjoy activities such as trampolining, holding water fights, and paintballing.

I am very keen on sport in general. I play basketball and go running every week. I also like swimming. At all times, I wear a *kirpan* – a short sword and symbol of my faith – under my clothes, and I carry this wherever I go. It is so important to me that I wear it when I go swimming, in the shower, and when I sleep."

Sikhs across the world

The number of Sikhs worldwide is estimated at almost 23 million, of whom over 18 million live in India.

INDIA
India is the home of Sikhism. The Harmandir Sahib (also known as the Golden Temple) is in Amritsar, India and is Sikhism's holiest building. Many Sikhs will have a picture of it in their homes, and will visit it if they go to India.

GREAT BRITAIN
Members of the 13th Southall Sikh scout group in west London, England. Formed in 1999, it was the first Sikh scout group in the U.K. Both boys and girls can join the group. Sikhs went to Britain from about 1900 but mainly after 1950.

NORTH AMERICA
An informal tabla (drum) lesson in the open air during a Sikh camp in Detroit, U.S.A. The boys are practicing, before playing during kirtan (songs praising God) in the evening at the campsite gurdwara. Sikhs went to North America from about 1900 onward.

What Do Sikhs Believe?

*"Sikh" comes from the Punjabi word **shishya**, which means "disciple" or "follower." Sikhs follow the teachings revealed by God to ten men known as "Gurus," who lived between 1469 and 1708 in an area known as the Punjab, on the Indian subcontinent.*

THE WORD "GURU" is a combination of two Punjabi words, *gu,* meaning "darkness," and *ru,* "light." A Guru is someone whom people believe can take away spiritual darkness and bring spiritual light. "Guru" has several different uses in Sikhism, for example: God; the ten human Gurus who were chosen to speak God's word; the sacred scripture, the *Guru Granth Sahib*; and the place of worship, the gurdwara.

What did the Gurus teach?

The Gurus' teaching can be summarized by the phrase "one God and one humanity." In India in the 1400s, men were divided into social groups called castes. Caste determined how important someone was believed to be and the kind of employment that that person could have. *Brahmins,* the highest caste, were the priests and political leaders; *sudras* were the servants. Women were

Sikhs bow before the Guru Granth Sahib as an act of respect for the sacred scriptures. They regard the Guru Granth Sahib as a living person – the living presence of God among God's people.

The Mul Mantra

Gurmukhi script	Transliteration	English
੧ੳ	ik onkar	One God
ਸਤਿਨਾਮੁ	satnam	True Name
ਕਰਤਾ ਪੁਰਖੁ	karta purakh	Creator
ਨਿਰਭਉ ਨਿਰਵੈਰੁ	nirbhau nirvair	Without fear, without hate
ਅਕਾਲ ਮੂਰਤਿ	akal murat	Without time, immanent
ਅਜੂਨੀ ਸੈਭੰ	ajuni saibhang	Without birth, self-illumined
ਗੁਰ ਪ੍ਰਸਾਦਿ	gur prasad	By the Guru's grace

Students of the tabla and harmonium learn to play their instruments. In gurdwaras today, kirtan is usually performed on tabla and harmonium. Kirtan is one of the ways in which Sikhs meditate on God's name.

not members of any caste, nor allowed to receive religious teaching, or read sacred scriptures. When a husband died, his wife was expected to commit suicide on his funeral pyre. But the Sikh Gurus taught that all people were equal and that everyone, regardless of their birth or gender, could receive religious teaching, and take part in religious services.

What do Sikhs believe about God?

Sikh teaching about God is summarized in the Mul Mantra – the first words of Guru Granth Sahib, the Sikh sacred scripture. These are also the first words of the *Japji Sahib*, one of the prayers that Sikhs say each morning.

Sikhs believe in one God, who created the world and is present in everything. Not only do all living beings – from people to animals such as insects – have God's *jot* (spiritual light) in them, but so too do inanimate objects. Sikhs believe in treating all people equally and in caring for the environment.

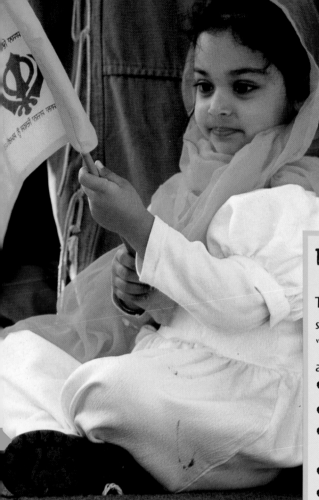

A young girl waving a small nishan sahib, the Sikh emblem. Sikhs believe that the jot (God's light) is in every living being and inanimate object.

The Five Ks

The five things that Sikhs wear to symbolize their faith all begin with "k" in the Punjabi language, so they are known as the "Five Ks":

- *kesh* (uncut hair)
- *kangha* (comb)
- *kara* (iron or steel bangle worn on the wrist)
- *kirpan* (sword)
- *kachhehra* or *kachs* (knee-length baggy shorts)

Do Sikhs believe in an afterlife?

Sikhs believe that all living beings and other objects have a beginning, an existence, and an end. When this physical existence finishes, Sikhs believe, God's *jot* within the being returns to earth in the form of another physical existence. This is called reincarnation, and is part of a constant cycle of birth, life, death, and rebirth.

Only those living things born as human beings can ever be liberated from the cycle. Then, the spiritual light that is in them returns permanently to God. Human beings can achieve this by obeying God's teachings in their daily lives. They can continually meditate on God's name, be honest in their daily lives, and give some of their earnings to help those in need, and serve God and other people.

How do Sikhs live their lives?

The Guru Granth Sahib warns Sikhs that they are living in an evil world and should not be corrupted by its many temptations. A Sikh should be like the lotus flower that only grows in stagnant, dirty water but whose flowers sit on the surface of the water and are white and clean. Sikhs are especially warned against two temptations – *haumai* and *maya*. Haumai is a combination of words

After death, Sikhs believe, the jot either comes back to earth in another form, whether living being or inanimate object, or returns to God.

for "I" and "me," and is often described as "ego." It is concerned with what "I" want, and not with obeying God's *hukam*, or will. Maya is the delusion of thinking that things such as money and possessions, which are temporary, are important, rather than obeying God, who is eternal.

What happens when a Sikh dies?

Before the funeral, the body is washed, clothed and, wearing the Five Ks – the five symbols of Sikh faith – is placed in a coffin. Sometimes the coffin is taken to the gurdwara to allow friends and relatives to pay their last respects. While the coffin is being carried, people in the funeral procession recite the mantras "Vahiguru" and "Satnam Vahiguru." The body is then cremated and the ashes are scattered in flowing water. Sometimes, after the funeral, the Guru Granth Sahib is read aloud in its entirety.

DEBATE – Can belief in reincarnation make people behave better?

- Yes. If people believe they may be punished in their next life for their bad behavior in this one, they may think carefully before behaving badly. They may also think that the quickest and easiest way out of the cycle of reincarnation is to obey God.

- No. People will always be selfish to some extent. Also, they only worry about the present, not about what might happen to them in years to come.

How Did Sikhism Start?

Sikhism as a formal religion can trace its origins back to the fifteenth century. It began with Guru Nanak, who came from the town of Talwandi, not far from Lahore, in what is today Pakistan.

GURU NANAK WAS born in 1469. His family were Hindus – followers of the traditional Indian religion of Hinduism. After his first day at school as a young child, Guru Nanak stated that the only learning that mattered to him was about God. When he was still a teenager, and working as a shopkeeper, people would come every evening to hear him teach about God. Gura Nanak would also share a meal with them, which he provided.

One morning, while he was bathing in a river, Gura Nanak was taken into God's presence. He was 30 years old. God told him to spend the rest of his life practicing *nam japna* (meditation on God's name) and teaching others to do the same. After this experience, Guru Nanak traveled around India and beyond, carrying out God's instructions. A musician called Mardana, who was a Muslim – a follower of the religion Islam – accompanied him.

Any person, Sikh or non-Sikh, may visit the Harmandir Sahib, the Golden Temple, and will be fed free of charge. The practice of eating a communal meal was started by Guru Nanak.

Guru Nanak, the first human Guru, who was taken into God's presence and given his life's work.

How did Guru Nanak know what to say?

Guru Nanak was told what to say by God, and would suddenly feel that God wished him to utter certain words. These words are known as *gurbani*, which comes from "Guru" and *bani*, meaning "word." To help people remember the gurbani, Mardana composed *raags* – traditional Indian tunes – to fit the words. Guru Nanak's followers used to meet together to sing the gurbani and listen to Guru Nanak's teaching.

How many Gurus were there?

There were nine more Gurus after Guru Nanak, making ten altogether. The last one was Guru Gobind Singh. God's jot (light) was in each of them, and their teachings were one and the same. To emphasize this, they are sometimes all called "Guru Nanak." So the first Guru is Guru Nanak 1, and his successors Guru Nanak 2, 3 and so on. On the anniversary of each Guru's birthday, a service that includes talks about his life is held at the gurdwara. On the birthday of the first Guru Nanak, a procession through the streets carrying the Guru Granth Sahib sometimes takes place, and friends and relatives exchange greetings cards. Cards are also sent out on Guru Gobind Singh's birthday.

Why were there ten Gurus?

If all of the Gurus' teachings were the same, why was there a need for ten Gurus one after another? Sikhs believe that everything that happens is according to God's will: there were ten Gurus because that is what God wanted. Another explanation is that God's teachings had to be revealed over many years so that people would be able to understand them properly. In a short time, only a limited amount of information can be understood.

Who were the ten Gurus?

The first Guru, Guru Nanak, died in 1539. His successor, Guru Angad, developed the practice of the *langar* (communal meal), which Guru Nanak had started. When Sikhs share a meal in this way, they are demonstrating their belief in the equality of all people. Guru Angad also devised the *gurmukhi* script, in which the Guru Granth Sahib is written. Guru Amar Das, who lived at the same time as Guru Nanak and Guru Angad, organized the Punjab into 22 districts, each with its own *masand* (local

ruler). He started the practice of the Guru meeting with Sikhs during the Indian festivals of Vaisakhi and Divali.

The fourth Guru, Guru Ram Das, founded a town in northern India, now called Amritsar, and uttered the *lavan*, the Sikh marriage hymn, as part of the gurbani (the word of God). Guru Arjan collected together all the gurbani God had given, and added the writings of some Hindu and Muslim holy men to show that God could be found in all religions. His collection is called the *Adi Granth*. He also supervised the building of the Harmandir Sahib, or Golden Temple, at Amritsar. In 1604, when the building was complete, Guru Arjan installed the Adi Granth inside, and bowed before the sacred scripture to show it was more important than he was. The following year, the new Mughul emperor, Jehangir, began to persecute Sikhs and others, and in 1606, Guru Arjan was killed as a martyr.

Guru Hargobind, who lived between 1595 and 1644, wore two swords: the *miri* and

Harmandir Sahib, in Amritsar, became known as the Golden Temple because of the gold plating that the Sikh Maharajah Ranjit Singh installed when Amritsar became part of his empire in 1802.

Sikhs believe that the teachings of the ten human Gurus, from Guru Nanak to Guru Gobind Singh, were one and the same. The sacred scripture, the Guru Granth Sahib, is the eternal Guru.

In a period of increasing persecution, Guru Har Rai, Hargobind's successor, continued to spread Sikh teachings. Guru Har Krishnan, who followed him, cared for people suffering from smallpox, and himself died of the disease. Guru Tegh Bahadur died a martyr's death defending the religious freedoms of Hindus and Sikhs, after Brahmins from Kashmir had sought his protection. Guru Gobind Singh, who was chosen by Guru Tegh Bahadur to succeed him, declared himself the last human Guru.

the *piri*. They represented his temporal and spiritual authority. To resist persecution, he trained Sikhs in military skills. He was imprisoned, and the occasion of his release is celebrated by Sikhs at the Divali festival. They hold fireworks displays, send greetings cards, and traditionally give sweets as presents.

A place for all

The Harmandir Sahib (Golden Temple) was designed to demonstrate some important Sikh teachings. A Muslim, Mian Mir, laid the foundation stone, showing respect for all religions. The building has entrances on all four sides, indicating that everyone is welcome. The steps leading down are a reminder that everyone should be humble before God. On the ground floor, the Guru Granth Sahib is installed. Upstairs, there is a balcony where people may sit undisturbed, listening to the kirtan which is played throughout the day.

How did the Sikh sacred scripture start?

The Guru Granth Sahib comprises the Adi Granth, which Guru Arjan placed in the Harmandir Sahib, and the gurbani given to Guru Tegh Bahadur by God. Shortly before Guru Gobind Singh died, he said that the Guru Granth Sahib would be the eleventh and last Guru and would be called by that name. In future, he said, if Sikhs wanted to know God's will, they should read this sacred scripture rather than ask a human Guru, as they had done before.

What is the Khalsa?

In 1699, when Sikhs gathered before Guru Gobind Singh at the festival of Vaisakhi, he stood there, sword in hand, asking who would "offer their head to the Guru." One by one, five Sikhs stepped forward to offer their heads, and one by one they were led into a tent. After the fifth volunteer was taken into the tent, they all emerged from the tent, alive and unharmed.

Guru Gobind Singh said these volunteers would be known as the *panj piare*, "the five beloved ones," because they were prepared to give their lives to the Guru. They became the first members of the Khalsa, a community of women and men who, because of their inner spirituality, have the courage to defend their Sikh faith and the human rights of others. Guru Gobind Singh also introduced the 5Ks – the five items worn by Sikhs to symbolize important Sikh teachings – and a daily code of conduct. In addition, he started the *amrit sanskar*, a ceremony of commitment in which Sikhs become members of the Khalsa.

Five Sikh boys, followed by five Sikh men, representing the panj piare, the five beloved ones, lead a procession of the Guru Granth Sahib to celebrate Vaisakhi.

Sikhs gather at the Harmandir Sahib in Amritsar, to listen to the reading of the Guru Granth Sahib. Sikhs do not refer to worship but to nam simran – meditation on God's name.

DEBATE - Does it help to remember the events of many years ago?

- Yes. It is possible to be inspired by other people's example. They can provide encouragement and give guidance about how to behave in certain situations.

- No. Times change. Expecting someone to act in the same way as people did years ago is unhelpful. It can also put pressure on people to behave in a way that they may not want to.

How are the "five beloved" remembered?

Today, to commemorate the events of 1699, gurdwaras are specially decorated for Vaisakhi and the *nishan sahib* – the flag that flies from the gurdwara – is changed. Sikhs will make an effort to attend the services, which will include talks about Guru Gobind Singh and the commitment of the panj piare. Traditionally, amrit sanskar ceremonies are held, and often there is a procession that conducts the Guru Granth Sahib through the streets.

A Sikh woman meditates on God's name, before a procession to celebrate Vaisakhi. When Sikhs went to the U.K. in the 1950s, the men went alone. Many were joined by their wives and families in the 1960s.

Why did Sikhs leave the Punjab?

From the time of the first Guru, Guru Nanak, Sikhs have been willing to live outside their traditional homeland. As early as the 1880s, when most of the Indian subcontinent was a British colony, some Sikhs left the Punjab to join the British army. After serving in the army, some returned to the Punjab, but others remained in Singapore or Hong Kong, where they had been sent by the British. Over the years, some of these Sikhs moved on to Indonesia and the Philippines, and later to Australia, Fiji, the U.S.A., and Canada.

At the end of the nineteenth century, about 32,000 Indian craftsmen, most of whom were Sikhs, left India to build a railway in Uganda. A little more than a fifth of them stayed in Kenya, Tanzania, and Uganda until the 1960s, when many left because of political upheavals in East Africa. They then moved mainly to Britain or North America.

Why did Sikhs come to Britain?

After the Second World War, Britain had a shortage of workers because many men had died in the fighting. Local government authorities and some large companies sent representatives to both the West Indies and the Indian subcontinent to encourage men to come and work in Britain. Many of those that answered the appeal were Sikhs.

In the words of one writer, these workers "helped first bandage up Britain's wounds of war and then set it on the road to recovery." Some of the Sikhs who made the move went to Scotland or the English Midlands, but many settled in west London. Today, the west London community numbers about 100,000 Sikhs and is the largest outside India.

How did they carry on their religion?

Britain's first gurdwara opened in 1911 in Putney, southwest London, England, and later moved to Shepherd's Bush in west London. The Sikhs who went to Britain before and soon after the Second World War found very few other gurdwaras. Many Sikhs often worked as many as 60 hours a week, and were too exhausted to travel a long way to a gurdwara afterwards. Sometimes they would meet in a nearby house or hire a local hall on a Sunday to practise nam simran (meditation on God's name). As more Sikhs arrived in Britain, and wives and families went over from India, they opened their own local gurdwaras. Usually, these were converted houses or shops, but now there are also purpose-built gurdwaras.

From small beginnings

The Singh Sabha gurdwara in Southall, west London, was founded by Sikhs who arrived in the 1950s. At first, they hired a local hall for kirtan on Sunday afternoons. Then, in 1961, a gurdwara was opened in a house, moving to a nearby hall as attenders increased. In 1967, the gurdwara moved to Havelock Road, converting a disused factory. It was extended in 1975. In 1999, the old gurdwara was demolished, and a new one, standing seven storeys high, was built to replace it. It is the largest gurdwara outside India.

Children learn about Sikh history and religion at a Sunday school run by the Ramgarhia Sabha gurdwara in Southall, west London. This gurdwara was started by Sikhs who went to the U.K. from Kenya in the 1960s.

How Do Sikhs Celebrate Their Faith?

There are no special holy days in Sikhism. Some Sikhs try to visit the gurdwara to pray every day. In the UK, many Sikhs will make a special effort to go to the gurdwara on a Sunday.

GURDWARAS NORMALLY OPEN daily at about four in the morning and close at about ten at night. The gurdwara can be visited at any time during these hours. Some Sikhs stay for only for a few minutes, others for several hours. Guru Amar Das said that Sikhs should rise at *amrit vela* (before dawn), as this is an especially spiritual time of the day. The daily services begin when the Guru Granth Sahib is carried down from a special room, where it has been

The nishan sahib, flying from the flag pole of the purpose-built gurdwara in Hounslow, west London. The symbol at the center of the flag reminds Sikhs that God is eternal and that they have a duty to serve both God and to care for all people.

The sacred scripture is installed on the takht (throne) and covered by a chianni (canopy). When the book is on the takht or being moved, a chauri is waved as a symbol of the authority of the Guru Granth Sahib.

Inside the gurdwara

"Gurdwara" comes from two Punjabi words: *Guru* and *duara*, which mean "doorway." A gurdwara is any place where the Guru Granth Sahib is kept. The presence of the book is the main reason why Sikhs visit the gurdwara. When they first pass through the doorway and enter the *diwan* (hall), they bow down before the Guru Granth Sahib, touching the floor with their forehead, and offer a gift, usually a small coin. In so doing, they show respect for the book. They then sit on the floor, taking care not to point their feet at the book, as this is a sign of disrespect.

taken to rest for the previous night. Some gurdwaras have a *granthi* – someone employed full time who reads aloud the Guru Granth Sahib to the *sangat* (congregation). But any Sikh, male or female, who can read the gurmukhi script, in which the Guru Granth Sahib is written, may read the sacred scripture.

Do services have a pattern?

After morning prayers, the granthi opens the Guru Granth Sahib at random and reads out the passage at the top of the left-hand page. This is called the *hukamnama*, and is God's message to the sangat for the day.

The first hukamnama of the day is usually written out and displayed so that people who arrive later can read it. After the hukamnama, those assembled stand up and, facing the Guru Granth Sahib, recite the prayer Ardas, during which requests to God may be made. Everyone then cups their hands to receive *karah parshad*, which is made from semolina, butter, and milk. Eating karah parshad symbolizes the Sikh belief in the equality of all people. This is followed by kirtan, which lasts for at least an hour and often much longer. There is also a *katha* (talk), based on the Guru Granth Sahib or an event or story from Sikh history.

How is a Sikh child given its name?

When a baby is only a few days old, the parents will go to the gurdwara to refer to the Guru Granth Sahib for guidance in the choice of name. There, the granthi prepares *amrit*, a mixture of water and sugar crystals, stirring the solution with a *khanda* (short, double-edged sword). At the same time, the granthi recites the first five verses of the Japji Sahib (morning prayer). He then wets the tip of a kirpan in the amrit he has prepared and touches the baby's tongue with it. The baby's mother drinks the rest of the amrit.

A name is chosen by opening the Guru Granth Sahib at random, reading aloud the passage at the top of the left-hand page, and selecting a name beginning with the first letter of the first word. The Sikh names "Kaur" (meaning princess) for a girl and "Singh" (meaning lion) for a boy are then added to the chosen name.

Sometimes a family that wishes to thank God for the gift of a new baby will arrange for an *Akhand Path* – a continuous reading of the Guru Granth Sahib from beginning to end. This takes 48 hours in total, each reader reading for two hours at a stretch. At the point of changeover, both readers will read a few lines together so there is no break in the reading. If family members can read the script of the Guru Granth Sahib, they are expected to take a turn reading. Otherwise, they listen to the readings. An Akhand Path reading may also be held to ask God's blessing for a forthcoming special event, such as a wedding, or moving house.

Shortly after a baby is born, the family consults the Guru Granth Sahib for guidance in choosing the first name. There is no difference between boys' and girls' names. The religious names of Singh for a boy and Kaur for a girl will be added.

Can the scripture be read at home?

Special arrangements have to be made if the Guru Granth Sahib is taken from the gurdwara into the home. The room where the scripture is to be kept must be cleaned, all furniture taken out, and a *takht* (throne) and *chianni* (canopy) put in the room. The family whose home it is will also prepare food, as visitors who come for the Akhand Path reading will be given *karah parshad* (which is made from semolina, butter, and milk), and the *langar* (communal meal). The end of the reading will be attended by as many family members and friends as possible.

DEBATE - Should children be given religious names?

* Yes. Religion is an important part of family life and parents try to bring up their children in their religion. It will help the children to closely identify with, and be proud of, their religion.

* No. Children should be left to choose their own beliefs when they are older. Later, they may want to change their religion. They may be bullied at school because of their name.

A modern painting, in traditional style, of a Sikh family house. Guru Nanak said that married life was the ideal, and the family is very important for Sikhs. Children are told stories about the Gurus by family members, and taught the daily prayers. Even very young children learn to repeat the Mul Mantra daily.

What is taking amrit?

Sikhs formally commit themselves to their faith through the ceremony of *amrit sanskar*, after which they become members of the Khalsa. Before taking amrit, as it is often called, a Sikh must wear the Five Ks and obey the Gurus' teachings in their daily lives. There is no minimum age for undergoing the ceremony, but the person should be old enough to understand the commitments that he or she is making.

Apart from those taking amrit, the only people present at the ceremony will be five Sikhs who symbolize the *panj piare* (the first five members of the Khalsa), a reader of the Guru Granth Sahib, and someone to make sure that the ceremony is not disturbed.

Amrit sanskar begins with the opening of the Guru Granth Sahib. One of the panj piare explains the Sikh teachings and the promises that the initiates will be making. A prayer is said, and the amrit prepared in a bowl made of iron or steel. As the *pastasas* (sugar crystals) are stirred into the water, using a khanda, the panj piare recite gurbani (God's words). The recitation takes about two hours. Then, one by one, the initiates come forward, kneel, and are given amrit to drink in their cupped hands. Amrit is then sprinkled five times on their hair and on their eyelids.

The initiates drink up any amrit that may be left, then each of them recites five times the Mul Mantra (opening words of the Guru Granth Sahib).

Guru Gobind Singh standing before those gathered at Anandpur Sahib on Vaisakhi in 1699. Sikhs believe that the institution of the Khalsa was introduced on that day and was the climax of the Gurus' teachings.

Symbols of the Sikh faith: kangha (comb), kara (iron or steel bangle worn on the wrist), kirpan (sword), kachhehra or kachs (knee-length baggy shorts), khanda (symbol of the Khalsa). Usually the kirpan is worn under a shirt or sweater, but on ceremonial occasions a longer kirpan, measuring about 3 feet, may be worn on the outside.

One of the panj piare then explains to the initiates the *rahit* (daily code of conduct) that they must follow.

Must a Sikh take amrit?

Guru Gobind Singh said that anyone who becomes a member of the Khalsa is a *sant-sipahi* – a person who obeys God's teachings and has the courage to challenge injustice.

Sikhs take amrit as an outward expression of their inner spirituality and commitment to God. But all Sikhs, whether or not they have taken amrit, should obey God's teachings in their daily lives.

DEBATE – Do ceremonies help people to keep commitments?

- Yes. To take part in a ceremony means you have seriously thought about your commitment. If, later, you find it difficult to keep the promises you made, other people who have also attended the ceremony can help you.

- No. If you are really committed to something, you should not need a ceremony. You may change your views later, and regret the promises you made. Then, you would either have to break them or pretend that you still believe in them when you no longer do.

Have Sikhs always had rules to obey?

From the time of Guru Nanak, Sikhs have been told that they should continually meditate on God's name; work honestly and give a proportion of what they earn to those in need; serve God and other people. In 1699, at the festival of Vaisakhi, Guru Gobind Singh introduced a *rahit* (daily code of conduct) for members of the Khalsa. Since then, there have been various versions of the Sikh codes of conduct, until the final authorized one – the *Rahit Maryada* – was approved by the Shiromani Gurdwara Parbandhak Committee (S.G.P.C.) on 3 February 1945.

What rules do Sikhs follow today?

The first part of the Rahit Maryada states that a Sikh is anyone who believes in one God; the ten human Gurus and their teachings; the Guru Granth Sahib; the importance of amrit sanskar. It also states that a Sikh may not belong to any other religion.

A Sikh should rise before dawn, says the Rahit Maryada and, after taking a bath, should recite the morning prayers. Before beginning a new task, a Sikh should pray to God for his blessing. Sikhs also have set prayers to say in the evening and before going to bed. The Rahit Maryada also emphasizes the importance of visiting the gurdwara, participating in the sangat, and listening to and meditating on the teachings of the Guru Granth Sahib.

During the day, everything a Sikh thinks and does should be according to the sacred scripture's teachings. A Sikh should learn the gurmukhi script so that he or she can read and understand the Guru Granth Sahib, and parents should teach their children about Sikh beliefs and practices.

Are there things Sikhs must not do?

There are four *kurahit* – things that Sikhs must never do. The first is to cut any bodily hair. The other prohibited actions are: the use of tobacco, alcohol or other drugs; commiting adultery; and eating halal meat – meat from animals killed in the manner laid down by Islam. Many Sikhs are vegetarian.

Sikhs making a gift of money to the Guru Granth Sahib. The money will be used to pay for the langar *(communal meal) and other free services provided to meet the needs of Sikhs and others*

What is the meaning of the Five Ks?

The Five Ks symbolize important Sikh teachings. For example, to keep your *kesh* (uncut hair) symbolizes obedience to God's will. Sikhs believe that hair is natural and given by God, so to cut your hair or shave your beard is breaking God's will. Guru Nanak said that Sikhs should die with their hair intact – "the hair with which they were born." To keep their hair covered, Sikh men, and some women, wear a turban. Other women wear a *chunni* (long scarf). You must cover your head in the gurdwara.

At a Sikh camp in Detroit, U.S.A. The two boys in the front, after playing sport, have showered and washed their hair, allowing it to dry naturally. Their hair is long, and they keep their heads covered.

The *kara* – the iron or steel bangle worn around the wrist – is a circle, which, like God, has no beginning or end. A circle is strong, so the kara is also a symbol of the strength and unity of the Khalsa. The *kangha* is the small comb used to comb the hair and to secure the kesh in place. It is a symbol that Sikhs should be neat, and tidy, and well-disciplined. The knee-length baggy shorts worn by Sikhs, called *kachhehra* or *kachhs*, symbolize the high moral standard of behavior that Sikhs must practice.

The *kirpan* (sword) symbolizes a Sikh's duty to uphold justice and defend those treated unjustly. It can be more than 3 feet in length, though most of those worn are between about 6 and 8 inches long. The word kirpan comes from two Punjabi words, *kirpa*, meaning "blessing" and *ana*, meaning "honor."

DEBATE – Should the law make exceptions, including for religious reasons?

- Yes. Society is enriched by religious beliefs and practices, and the law should be flexible about these. History has shown that intolerance can often lead to persecution.
- No. Everyone should follow the same set of laws. If special laws are made for one group of people, other groups will want special laws to be made for them too. This could lead to chaos.

Is wearing a kirpan unlawful?

The Criminal Justice Act, passed by the British government in 1988, generally made it illegal to carry a bladed or pointed instrument. Section 139 of the Act provided for certain exceptions, including for religious reasons. A Sikh may lawfully carry a kirpan in the U.K.. Since the attacks on New York's World Trade Center in 2001, airlines have insisted, for security reasons, that Sikhs put their kirpan in their hold luggage and not wear it during the flight.

A Sikh woman wearing a kirpan and kara.

What happens at a Sikh wedding?

The *anand karaj* (wedding ceremony) takes place in the presence of the Guru Granth Sahib. It is the Guru Granth Sahib that is the witness to the marriage, not the people attending the ceremony. The bride and bridegroom show their agreement to their union by bowing before the sacred scripture. The prayer Ardas is said, and the bride's father places garlands of flowers around the Guru Granth Sahib and around the necks of the bride and groom.

The *lavan* (circling) then takes place. The bride's father gives one end of the bride's *chunni* (scarf) to the groom, who leads the bride in walking around the Guru Granth Sahib while first the *ragis* (musicians) and then the *sangat* (congregation) sing the four verses of the marriage hymn from the Guru Granth Sahib. The Ardas is repeated, and other prayers are recited. The Guru Granth Sahib is then opened at random to find verses that will give God's guidance to the couple, and karah parshad is distributed to the sangat. Sometimes, the bride and groom join the ragis and perform kirtan, to praise God at the start of their married life.

Can Sikhs marry whomever they like?

The Rahit Maryada (the Sikh code of conduct) includes the statement that a Sikh should marry another Sikh. Apart from this, the choice of marriage partner lies with the couple themselves, and their decision will be respected by their parents. Traditionally parents suggest, but do not insist on, a partner, in what is known as an "assisted marriage."

The bride and bridegroom bow before the Guru Granth Sahib to show that they agree to the marriage. The Guru Granth Sahib, the living presence of God, is the witness to the wedding.

Young mothers and their children at a gurdwara. Families have an important role in marriages, and traditionally assist in the choice of the marriage partner. The final decision about whether to marry is made by the prospective marriage partners themselves.

How important is marriage?

Marriage is very important in Sikhism. Guru Nanak taught that family life was the ideal kind of life. For a Sikh to remain single throughout his or her life is unusual. In the Guru Granth Sahib, marriage is seen as the joining together of the jot (God's light) in the two people. The sacred scripture says: *They are not man and wife who have only physical contact. Only those are truly married who have one spirit in two bodies.*

Can Sikhs get divorced?

Most Sikhs accept that sometimes marriages do break down. When this happens, both families will support the couple as best they can and try to help them overcome any difficulties. If it is obvious that the marriage is beyond repair, the couple may divorce. Divorcees are allowed to marry again.

How Do Sikhs Regard Modern Issues?

*Guru Nanak taught that Sikhs should both serve God and help everyone else, whatever their religion or country of origin. This is the concept of **seva** – "service" or "voluntary help."*

TO SIKHS, SERVING God by, for example, reading the Guru Granth Sahib in the gurdwara, and helping other people are both equally important.

The nishan sahib flag that flies from a gurdwara signifies that any person, Sikh or other, will be given accommodation for a night and a meal free of charge.

The 13th Sikh Scout Group in Southall, west London. Members take part in many celebrations, including the 300th anniversary of the Khalsa, held at the Royal Albert Hall, London, and attended by Prince Charles.

Every gurdwara offers *langar*, a communal meal that is served whenever the gurdwara is open. Traditionally, people eat this meal sitting cross-legged on the floor, but usually a few tables are available for the elderly and those with young children. Some people, and not just Sikhs, visit the gurdwara every day for their main meal. The langar provides opportunities for people of all ages to perform seva (voluntary help) by, for example, cooking or serving the food, or afterward cleaning the pots and pans. Because of this, the Rahit Maryada describes the langar as the "laboratory of seva."

Men preparing the communal meal, the langar, at a gurdwara.

Gurdwaras help both Sikhs and non-Sikhs in other ways too. For example, a gurdwara in Hounslow, west London, organizes a sponsored walk every year, to pay for eye clinics in India. It has also encouraged its members to register as bone marrow donors to help sick people in Britain. Gurdwaras also arrange to help people with financial or legal problems, as well as those who are unemployed and looking for jobs.

Where do Sikhs do voluntary work?

Seva can be done anywhere and can include many different kinds of service. In 1998, a Sikh Scout group was started in Southall to meet the needs of young people. Although the leaders of the troop are all Sikhs, boys and girls of any religion are welcome to join.

In 1999, to celebrate the 300th anniversary of the Khalsa, a group of young people in west London founded Khalsa Aid. This is a humanitarian relief organization that helps people across the world, regardless of their religion or ethnic background.

DEBATE – Should voluntary organizations care for the sick and the elderly?

- Yes. People should be willing to give some of their time or money to charities involved in helping others. Governments of countries have only limited funds, and should spend money only on things that voluntary organizations cannot provide.

- No. So long as voluntary organizations are doing the job of caring for people, governments will think they have no responsibility to provide for them. People pay taxes to the government, and these ought to go toward paying for their own care, when it is needed, and the care of others.

In a gurdwara in west London, women participate in a Sikh service alongside men. Girls receive a similar education to boys in religious and secular studies.

Do Sikhs believe in women's equality?

Sikhs believe in one God and one humanity. The Guru Granth Sahib teaches that women and men are equal in both religious and worldly matters.

Guru Nanak said that both women and men could achieve union with God. The love that a woman has for her husband, he said, is an example of the love of a Sikh for God. He emphasized the importance of women in giving birth to, and caring for, rulers and kings. He also denied the belief, sometimes held, that giving birth made a woman ritually polluted for a certain number of days.

Guru Amar Das appointed women as religious teachers. When Guru Gobind Singh founded the Khalsa, he asked his wife to place sugar crystals in the amrit water. To Hindus of the time, asking a woman to do this would be seen as making the amrit religiously polluted. But Sikhs did not believe this. Both women and men were eligible to become members of the Khalsa, and both had to obey the same rules.

Are women equal to men in practice?

Any role, or post of responsibility, in the Sikh community may be held by a woman or a man. In India in 1999, a woman, Bibi Jagjir Kaur, was elected president of the Shiromani Gurdwara Prabandhak Committee, the organization with legal responsibility for the care and management of all gurdwaras in the Punjab. In the UK, women have been elected members of gurdwara management committees, and in some cases have also been chosen as president.

However, the majority of posts on the management committee are held by men. Women are often responsible for women's meetings or education, but are not usually given more public positions such as president or General Secretary. Even though both women and men may read from the Guru Granth Sahib in a gurdwara, no woman has ever been appointed as a full-time granthi. Women are often found doing the more domestic tasks in the gurdwara while men occupy the more prominent roles. It has been argued that this is a reflection of the male-dominated culture found in the Punjab and, to a lesser extent, in the U.K. today. But it is not what the Guru Granth Sahib teaches.

DEBATE – Should all people be treated equally?

- Yes. People should not be penalized because of their individuality. In today's society, people should be allowed to do what they want as long as it does not harm or injure other people.

- No. Different people have different needs. If everyone was treated equally, it would be unfair to those most in need. If people work harder, or are more skilled, than others, then they are entitled to receive higher rewards than those who make less effort.

Kirtan is often sung to the accompaniment of the tabla and harmonium in the gurdwara. At a congregational meeting, kirtan may last from one to several hours.

Do Sikhs practise birth control?

Sikhs believe in maintaining the body's natural form, so they will not undergo surgery as a method of birth control. For example, vasectomies (surgery to make a man sterile), or the removal of the womb or ovaries, are forbidden unless they are for health reasons. There are no Sikh teachings against other forms of birth control, but contraception is allowed only within marriage. Sex is regarded as an expression of love between a husband and wife, and not as wholly or mainly to have children.

Living together as husband and wife, but without formally marrying, is not acceptable. For young people to have sexual relations before marriage is completely against Sikh teaching. Even young people dating members of the opposite sex is not allowed, unless they go out with a group of friends, which would usually be acceptable. But if they were going to a disco or a party on their own, parents would be concerned.

Can Sikhs have abortions?

There is no Sikh teaching specifically on abortion, but Sikhs are taught to respect all life. They believe that life begins at fertilization and is sacred. Abortion is therefore morally wrong. But although Sikhs find abortion unacceptable, even if the child may be born physically or mentally disabled, they also recognize

A Sikh mother gives birth in a hospital.

A Sikh family in Delhi, dressed in a mix of western and Sikh clothing.

DEBATE - Should there be a limit on family size?

* Yes. The world is overpopulated, there are too many mouths to feed, and there are famines in different parts of the world. It raises the dignity of humanity if families limit the number of children they have.

* No. Famines are not caused by overpopulation, but by civil war and the unfair distribution of food and other resources due to the greed of the richer countries. In countries such as the UK, low birth rate is a concern, not having too many children.

the right of parents to make their own decisions. If the pregnancy is the result of rape, some Sikhs consider that an abortion may be justified.

Sikhs have always been opposed to the use of amniocentesis (examination of the embryo) to establish the gender of the unborn child. In some cultures, a son is seen to be of greater importance than a daughter, and if the fetus is female the family may want an abortion. Such a practice is illegal in India, and Sikhs regard it as infanticide (child murder). The Rahit Maryada says that Sikhs should not associate with anyone who practices infanticide. In any case, Sikhs believe that both males and females are of equal worth.

How do Sikhs view modern medicine?

From the time of the Gurus, Sikhs have been involved in caring for the sick. Guru Nanak is said to have healed people suffering from leprosy, an infectious disease that in the fifteenth century was incurable. Guru Arjan founded a hospital to care for lepers.

In the modern world, it is acceptable for Sikhs to donate their bodies for use in transplant surgery. This is because of the Sikh belief that, when someone dies, that person's jot (divine light) leaves the body and has no more use for it. The Guru Granth Sahib says: "The dead may be cremated or buried, or thrown to the dogs, or cast into the waters, or down an empty well. No one knows where the soul goes and disappears to." In 1987 a Sikh established the "Life After Death Society" in Calcutta to encourage people to donate their bodies for transplant surgery and medical research after their death.

In India, blindness due to damage to the cornea is a serious problem. The Guru Ram Das Mission in the U.K. financially supports hospitals and eye clinics in the Punjab. Eye clinics in India have also been sponsored for several years by a west London gurdwara in Hounslow. The gurdwara has also organized meetings to encourage its members to donate bone marrow.

Sikhs with various disabilities are cared for at an institute for education and welfare in India. Sikhs accept that medical treatment may be necessary to help ease or save a person's life.

Studying the human genetic code. Sikhs accept that research advances medicine but they oppose manipulation of genes.

Not all medical practices are acceptable to Sikhs. Artificial insemination, for example, is permitted only if the husband's sperm and wife's egg are used. The use of donor eggs or sperm is regarded as no better than adultery.

What about genetic engineering?

Many Sikhs would consider that altering the structure of human cells, even if it is done to prevent the spread of a genetic illness, is wrong. If life begins at fertilization, then genetic engineering is altering the living form that God has given. Some Sikhs, however, disagree and believe that such medical knowledge is God-given and should be used to help people.

DEBATE - Are there limits beyond which medicine should not go?

- Yes. Once the D.N.A .(genetic code) of an individual is altered, the process cannot be reversed, or its effects foreseen. Cloning (making a genetically identical being) should also be prohibited. A clone may have the same D.N.A., but it will not be an exact duplicate because it will not have the same personality.

- No. Limits may prevent cures being found for diseases such as A.I.D.S. and cancer. Limits should not be put on medical research just because a few people may misuse it.

Do Sikhs think drug-taking is wrong?

Tobacco, alcohol, and drugs are forbidden to Sikhs. In Guru Nanak's time, taking drugs was common. The Mughul emperor Babur once offered Guru Nanak a drink containing opium. He refused, saying that he was "hooked" on God's name. Not only do drugs and alcohol damage your own body, Sikhs say, but they also hurt other people, as shown in the numbers of deaths and injuries caused by drunk drivers.

Do Sikhs think suicide is wrong?

Sikhs believe that life is given by God, so taking your own life is wrong. Guru Nanak said: "God sends us and we take birth. God calls us back and we die." The Gurus strongly condemned the Hindu practice of their day whereby women threw themselves on their husband's burning funeral pyre.

The Gurus taught that Sikhs have a temporal, as well as a spiritual duty. They should care for their physical bodies, maintaining the body in its natural state, by not cutting or shaving body hair, unless this is necessary for a medical operation.

Is euthanasia allowed?

Generally, Sikhs believe that euthanasia, or "mercy" killing – killing someone to put an end to his or her pain and suffering – is wrong. But, if someone is terminally ill, many Sikhs think that aggressive medical treatment

India's Harbajan Singh leaps with delight after bowling out an English cricketer during a Test Match. Drug-taking in sports is becoming common, and this is a new challenge facing Sikh sportsmen and women.

Sikhs perform martial arts exercises. Any activity that keeps the body in a good, natural, physical and mental state is encouraged by Sikhs.

just to delay that person's death is inappropriate. Some Sikhs would argue that, as long as there were medical and legal safeguards to ensure that the patient was requesting euthanasia, it should be allowed if the person's quality of life had become very poor.

DEBATE - Is quality of life more important than life itself?

- Yes. All people are entitled to dignity and self-respect. If people lose these things through advanced age or illness they should be able to choose to end their life. Some people, such as those in a coma for years, have lost their personal identity and will never recover. They should be put out of their misery.

- No. Life is not there for any person to take away, even if it is your own life. Many people who suffer provide an inspiration to others, leading them to undertake humanitarian work for the benefit of others.

How Are Sikhs Responding To The Challenges Of Today?

The Gurus taught that Sikhs should earn their living honestly, and be kind and generous to others.

IN SIKHISM, THERE is no idea of renouncing the world and living life as an ascetic, or of begging. The Guru Granth Sahib says: "He alone has found the right way who eats what he earns through toil and shares his earnings with the needy."

When Guru Nanak chose to eat at the home of the carpenter, Bhai Lalo, rather than with Malik Bhago, the local Muslim leader, Malik Bhago was upset. Asked to explain his behaviour, Guru Nanak said that Bhai Lalo earned his living honestly whereas Malik Bhago made his money by exploiting the poor.

Guru Nanak established a Sikh community at Kartarpur that lived according to his teachings. Although he was Guru, he set an example to his community by doing manual labor in the afternoon. Sikhs that do not have paid employment can do seva (service) in the gurdwara or other voluntary work.

Guru Nanak also taught that "Truth is high, but higher still is truthful living." There are therefore some jobs that a Sikh should not do. According to the Rahit Maryada, a Sikh should not indulge in gambling or use alcohol, tobacco, or

A Sikh judge in London. Law is a profession highly regarded by Sikhs.

The Sikh star player in the film Bend it like Beckham. *There is much discussion about why there are so few Sikh soccer players.*

Between two cultures

In 2001 the film *Bend it like Beckham* was released. It shows how young Sikhs whose families had come to the U.K. from Nairobi, Kenya, in the 1960s live between the two cultures of British society and their Sikh faith. The film tells the story of a Sikh girl who supports Manchester United and dreams of playing professional football. At first her family are worried about her ambition, but later she receives their support in realizing her dream.

drugs, so any employment involving them should be avoided. Some Sikhs do own or work in shops that sell tobacco or alcohol. Other Sikhs, including those that have taken amrit, would not do those jobs.

What do Sikhs do for recreation?

Harmeet Kaur, the dental student introduced on page 4, attended a Sikh camp where there was paintballing, trampolining, and water fights. She also played a variety of sports and went swimming, wearing her kirpan at all times. Sport is popular with Sikhs. The Indian national cricket and hockey teams usually have one or more Sikh members. Currently, a Sikh professional footballer plays for Leeds United Football Club. Sikhs also enjoy going to the cinema or to a concert, but would not go to places such as discotheques.

Sikhs stand guard outside the Harmandir Sahib (Golden Temple) during times of political and social unrest.

Do Sikhs condone violence?

Sikhs have a reputation as brave fighters. According to the teachings of the Gurus, Sikhs have a responsibility not only for the spiritual, but also for the temporal – what takes place in the world. But it was not until Guru Hargobind became Guru in 1606, after the martyrdom of Guru Arjan, that Sikhs had a standing army. This army was not for starting a war, but for protecting Sikhs who were being persecuted. When the Hindu Brahmins asked for Guru Tegh Bahadur's protection, the Guru went to see the Mughul emperor to intercede for them, but he did not take an army with him.

Guru Gobind Singh led his army in many battles against the Mughuls, but

Dharam yudh – Guru Gobind Singh's just war principles

● War should be used only as a last resort, when all other efforts to find peace have failed.

● No war should be started out of anger or for revenge.

● Any property taken during a war must be returned afterward, looting is strictly forbidden, and no territory captured should be kept after the war.

● The army should be made up of only paid soldiers, who must obey the Sikh code of conduct.

● Women should at all times be treated with respect.

● Only the minimum of force needed should be used, and the war should be stopped once its aim is achieved.

only because Sikhs were being attacked. Guru Gobind Singh further introduced *dharam yudh* – the just war theory – to limit the scale of death and injury. In one battle, a Sikh, Bhai Khanaiya, was seen tending wounded soldiers in both the Sikh and the Mughul armies. He was brought before Guru Gobind Singh to explain his actions. But the Guru praised Bhai Khanaiya for caring for all the injured, not just those on his own side.

Guru Gobind Singh emphasized that any war fought by Sikhs must be a just one. "I have no ambition but to wage righteous war," he said. The kirpan that Sikhs wear is a reminder of God's care for them, and of their duty to care for those that are discriminated against or treated unfairly.

DEBATE – Is it ever right to use violence?

- Yes. There are occasions when violence is the only answer. If someone is about to kill someone else, or a group of people, or if one country is threatening to bomb and kill people in another country, there may be no alternative but to use violence.

- No. Violence leads to even more violence. When a country threatened with violence responds with violence, this often leads to a war that might never have taken place. People like Mahatma Gandhi in India and Martin Luther King in the U.S.A. have shown that you can achieve your aims using non-violent methods.

A British Sikh officer cadet demonstrates a laser rangefinder. The British Army encourages people of all faiths to join its ranks. The Police Force, too, recruits many Sikhs.

Do Sikhs respect other religions?

Sikhs believe that God can be found in all religions. Guru Gobind Singh said, "Hindus and Muslims are one. The same Being is creator and nourisher of all. Recognize no distinction between them." The sacred Sikh scripture, the Guru Granth Sahib, includes the *bhagat bani* – words of Hindu and Muslim holy men.

From the time of the Gurus, Sikhism has taught respect for the right of people to worship God according to their own faith. When Guru Nanak said, "There is neither Hindu nor Muslim, therefore whose path shall I follow? I shall follow God's path," he was not criticizing Hinduism or Islam, but people who

A summit on religion and the environment in Atami, Japan, in March 1995. Sikhs believe that God created the world and that they have a responsibility to care for the environment.

Sikhs meeting with student teachers of religious education in Southall, London. Sikhs welcome opportunities to explain their faith to other people, but do not try to convert people to Sikhism.

perform religious actions without ever thinking in any way about God. Guru Nanak believed that what was important was a person's individual relationship with God.

On many occasions, the Gurus defended people of other religions. For example, Guru Amar Das persuaded the Mughul government to remove a tax on Hindu pilgrims visiting the holy city of Hardwar. Guru Hargobind obtained the release of Hindu princes who had been unjustly imprisoned, before he would accept his own freedom. Guru Tegh Bahadur was respected by the Hindu Brahmins from Kashmir as a religious leader who was prepared to defend their own freedom of worship. The help that he gave them, against Mughal Emperor Aurangzeb of northern India, led to his martyrdom.

Are people of other faiths welcome?

Sikhs have always made people of all faiths welcome. When the Mughul Emperor Akbar visited Guru Amar Das, he was told to eat langar, before meeting the Guru. The Harmandir Sahib (Golden Temple) in Amritsar was designed with four main entrances, emphasizing that anyone may enter. The foundation stone for the building was laid by Mian Mir, a local Muslim leader, at the invitation of Guru Arjan.

Anyone can attend a gurdwara, and people of different faiths may be invited to address the sangat on matters of general interest. Seva (service) is also available to anyone who needs it, not just Sikhs. The kirpan worn by Sikhs reminds them of their duty to uphold the rights of all people, whatever their faith or beliefs.

Do Sikhs have an environmental policy?

The Mul Mantra says that God both created the world and is present in all creation. The Guru Granth Sahib states: "I see the Creator pervading everywhere." The sacred scripture also teaches that the world comes into being through God's will. The present tense is used, as Sikhs believe that creation is a continuous process that is ongoing. Thus, people have a responsibility to care for other living beings and to treat the environment with respect.

Puran Singh, who founded Pingalwala (a home for the sick and disabled) in Amritsar, typifies this caring attitude. As early as the 1960s, he protested against government policies, such as deforestation, that harmed the environment and deprived local villagers of the fuel they needed for cooking. To remain free to attack such policies, Puran Singh refused government support for his humanitarian work.

Today, the wealth of the Indian state of Punjab is based on agriculture, as Sikhs, like others, have made full use of modern technological developments. The use of high-yielding crops has brought economic prosperity, but created environmental problems. The Punjab is a land with five rivers, and a system of irrigation canals that carry the water to the fields. Now, the water level has fallen so much that the bore wells supplying fresh water to the villages need to be dug much deeper. Also, the

Sikhs enjoying a canoe ride during their time spent at a camp site in Detroit, U.S.A. Such camps, which are organized by Sikhs for Sikhs, offer opportunities for both recreation and learning.

Although the Sikh code of conduct does not forbid hunting game or eating meat, most Sikhs are vegetarian. Because langar is for everyone, the food served will be vegetarian, and will not contain egg, because eating eggs can be seen as eating a potential life.

A model Sikh

Puran Singh was born in 1904 and dedicated his life to seva (service). In 1934, while doing seva in Lahore (now in Pakistan), he found an abandoned baby who was disabled. From then on, he cared for the child, whom he called Piara Singh, carrying him on his back as he went around helping others. In 1947 he founded Pingalwala, meaning "home for the disabled," which cares for people who are sick, disabled or dying. In 1992 Puran Singh was nominated for the Nobel Peace Prize. He died in 1993, but his work continues.

use of artificial fertilizers has harmed the soil and threatens to pollute the rivers. To make matters worse, the use of genetically modified seeds has made farmers more dependent on fertilizers and ruined some of them financially.

Do Sikhs disapprove of hunting?

By Guru Hargobind's time – the seventeenth century – the Gurus were both spiritual and temporal, or worldly, leaders. So, it was not unusual for them to go hunting, and there are accounts of Guru Hargobind and Guru Gobind Singh doing so. Sikhs believe deliberately causing suffering to another living being is wrong, and condemn the cruelty of activities such as bear-baiting. But they would leave a decision on hunting to the conscience of the individual.

REFERENCE

Sikh population

World population	22 874 000
India	18 360 000
Indian state of Punjab	11 000 000
U.S.A.	500 000
U.K.	336 000
Canada	147 000
Malaysia	50 000
Singapore	20 000
Australia	12 000
Latin America	9 000
New Zealand	2 817

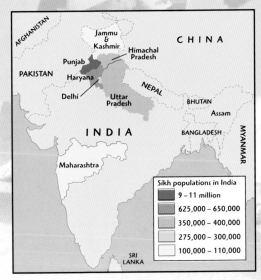

Sikh populations in India
- 9 – 11 million
- 625,000 – 650,000
- 350,000 – 400,000
- 275,000 – 300,000
- 100,000 – 110,000

By far the greatest majority of Sikhs live in and around the Indian subcontinent. The largest number of Sikhs to be found outside Asia and southeast Asia live in the U.S.A.

Timeline of Sikhism

1469 Birth of Guru Nanak.

1499 Guru Nanak taken into God's presence and given his life's work of meditating on God's name, and teaching others to do the same.

1538–39 Death of Guru Nanak, who was succeeded by Lahina, known as Guru Angad.

1552 Death of Guru Angad and succession of Guru Amar Das.

1574 Death of Guru Amar Das and succession of Guru Ram Das.

1581 Death of Guru Ram Das and succession of Guru Arjan.

1603–04 Compilation of the Adi Granth under the supervision of Guru Arjan.

1604 Completion of the Harmandir Sahib (Golden Temple) in Amritsar, and installation of the Adi Granth by Guru Arjan.

1606 Martyrdom of Guru Arjan and succession of Guru Hargobind.

1644 Death of Guru Hargobind and succession of Guru Har Rai.

1661 Death of Guru Har Rai and succession of Guru Har Krishnan.

1664 Death of Guru Har Krishnan and succession of Guru Tegh Bahadur.

1675 Martyrdom of Guru Tegh Bahadur and succession of Guru Gobind Singh.

1699 Introduction of the institution of the Khalsa by Guru Gobind Singh at Anandpur Sahib on the festival of Vaisakhi.

1708 Death of Guru Gobind Singh and succession of the Guru Granth Sahib, ending the line of human Gurus.

1801 Ranjit Singh becomes sovereign, or Maharajah, of the Sikh state of Punjab and supervises the gold plating and marble facing of the Harmandir Sahib.

1909 Anand Marriage Act passed, stating that the Anand Karaj is the only approved order for Sikh marriages.

1919 Jallianwala Bagh Massacre in Amritsar, near the Harmandir Sahib. Some 1200 Sikhs killed, and many more injured, when British army troops fired on a peaceful crowd of Sikhs gathered there.

1925 Sikh Gurdwaras Act passed in India, giving the Sikh community responsibility for managing gurdwaras in the Punjab. The Shiromani Gurdwara Parbandhak Committee, established in 1920, is chosen by the Sikhs to have this responsibility.

1947 Partition of the Punjab, following Indian independence from the U.K., resulting in mass migration of Hindus and Sikhs from Pakistan, and of Muslims from Indian Punjab. Many Sikh sacred places, including Guru Nanak's birthplace of Talwandi, now in Pakistan Punjab.

1984 The Indian army, acting on the orders of prime minister Indira Gandhi, attack the Harmandir Sahib complex on 4 June. Jarnail Singh Bhindranwale, the leading campaigner for an independent Sikh state, is among those killed in the attack. On 31 October Indira Gandhi is assassinated, allegedly by one of her Sikh bodyguards, leading to a massacre of Sikhs, particularly in Delhi and New Delhi.

The Six Major Faiths

BUDDHISM
Founded
535 B.C.E. in northern India

Number of followers
Estimated at 360 million

Holy Places
Bodh Gaya, Sarnath, both in northern India

Holy Books
The Tripitaka

Holy Symbol
Eight-spoked wheel

JUDAISM
Founded
In what is now Israel, around 2000 B.C.E.

Number of followers
Around 13 million religious Jews

Holy Places
Jerusalem, especially the Western Wall

Holy Books
The Torah

Holy Symbol
Seven-branched menorah (candle stand)

CHRISTIANITY
Founded
Around 30 C.E., Jerusalem

Number of followers
Just under 2 000 million

Holy Places
Jerusalem and other sites associated with the life of Jesus

Holy Books
The Bible (Old and New Testaments)

Holy Symbol
Cross

HINDUISM
Founded
Developed gradually in prehistoric times

Number of followers
Around 750 million

Holy Places
River Ganges, especially at Varanasi (Benares). Several other places in India

Holy Books
Vedas, Upanishads, Mahabharata, Ramayana

Holy Symbol
Aum

SIKHISM
Founded
Northwest India, 15th century C.E.

Number of followers 22.8 million

Holy Places
There are five important, takhts, or seats of high authority: in Amritsar, Patna Sahib, Anandpur Sahib, Nanded, and Talwandi.

Sacred Scripture
The Guru Granth Sahib

Holy Symbol
The Khanda, the symbol of the Khalsa.

ISLAM
Founded
610 C.E. in Arabia (modern Saudi Arabia)

Number of followers
Over 1000 million

Holy Places
Makkah and Madinah, in Saudi Arabia

Holy Books
The Qur'an

Holy Symbol
Crescent and star

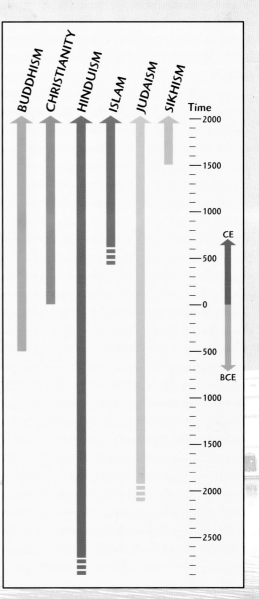

While some faiths can point to a definite time and person for their origin, others cannot. For example, Muslims teach that the beliefs of Islam predate Muhammad and go back to the beginning of the world. Hinduism apparently developed from several different prehistoric religious traditions.

GLOSSARY

amrit sanskar The ceremony at which Sikhs become members of the Khalsa.

anand karaj Sikh marriage ceremony in the presence of the Guru Granth Sahib.

Bhagat bani The writings of Hindu and Muslim holy men that have been included in the Guru Granth Sahib.

dastar A turban worn by men, and some women, to cover uncut hair.

diwan Literally "court," the hall in the gurdwara where the Guru Granth Sahib is installed.

five Ks The five items worn by Sikhs to symbolize important teachings: kesh (uncut hair), kangha (comb), kara (iron or steel bangle worn on the wrist), kirpan (sword), and kachhehra or kachs (knee-length baggy shorts).

granthi Any woman or man who reads the Guru Granth Sahib.

Gurbani Literally "God's word;" the words divinely given to the human Gurus, which are today found in the Guru Granth Sahib.

gurdwara Literally "doorway to the Guru;" the Sikh place of worship, anywhere that the Guru Granth Sahib is installed, whether a purpose-built building or one converted from another use, a room in a home or a tent in a field.

Gurmukhi Literally, "from the mouth of the Guru," the special script in which the Guru Granth Sahib is written.

Guru Granth Sahib The Sikhs' sacred scripture; God's living presence among God's people.

Harmandir Sahib The most important Sikh gurdwara, located in Amritsar in the Punjab; also known as the "Golden Temple" because of the gold plating on its dome and upper storey.

haumai A combination of the Punjabi for "I" or "me," often translated as "ego."

hukam God's will or divine order; the belief that all things happen according to God's will.

hukamnama God's word or command, addressed to those present at a gurdwara service.

jot God's light, which is present in all living beings and inanimate objects.

kachhehra/kachs Knee-length baggy shorts; one of the Five Ks.

kangha A small comb worn in the hair; one of the Five Ks.

kara An iron or steel bangle worn around the wrist; one of the Five Ks.

Khalsa A community of women and men who, because of their spirituality, have the courage to defend their Sikh faith and the human rights of others.

Khalsa Aid A humanitarian organization, started in 1999 by Sikhs from the west London and Slough areas, that takes relief aid to people in different countries regardless of their religion or ethnic origin.

khanda A short, double-edged sword; also the name of the symbol of the Khalsa – a circle with a two-edged sword in the center and two crossed kirpan, one on either side.

kirat karo To work honestly and give a proportion of what you earn to the poor; one of the responsibilities of all Sikhs.

kirpan A sword; one of the Five Ks.

kirtan Literally means "songs praising God;" passages from the Guru Granth Sahib and other approved writers that are set to *raags*. One of the most important ways that Sikhs meditate on God's name.

Kurahit Literally "prohibition;" four actions forbidden for Khalsa Sikhs: cutting body hair; using tobacco, alcohol, or other drugs; committing adultery; eating halal meat.

langar The communal meal that is available to everyone at a gurdwara.

Lavan Literally "circling," the four verses of the marriage hymn that are sung at a Sikh wedding while the bridegroom leads the bride in circling the Guru Granth Sahib.

mantra A syllable, word or phrase, that is repeated while concentrating on it, leading, it is believed, to a higher level of spiritual experience.

Masand Local officials appointed by the Guru to give religious teaching, to collect offerings of money given to the Guru, and to supervise local sangats.

Maya The delusion of attachment to temporal things, as opposed to attachment to God.

Mul Mantra Literally "root" or "seed" mantra, a summary of Sikh teaching about God, the first verse of the Guru Granth Sahib and of the Japji Sahib, a prayer recited by Sikhs each morning.

nam japna The continual meditation on God's name, one of the responsibilities of all Sikhs.

nishan sahib The triangular flag flown outside a gurdwara. It is usually saffron in color, although it may be dark blue. The Khanda, the symbol of the Khalsa, is shown on it.

panj piare Literally "beloved ones," the five Sikhs who offered their heads to the Guru at the festival of Vaisakhi in 1699.

raag A traditional Indian musical mode, or tune, aimed at putting people in the right emotion to hear and understand the words said.

ragi Musicians who accompany the singing of kirtan.

Rahit Maryada The Sikh code of conduct published by the Shiromani Gurdwara Parbandhak Committee on 3 February 1945 and followed by most Sikhs.

sangat Literally "being together" or "congregation," a gathering of Sikhs to practice nam japna (meditation on God's name); any Sikh community that meets together at a local gurdwara.

seva Literally "service," whether service to God by, for example, reading the Guru Granth Sahib, performing kirtan or helping in the langar by giving, cooking and serving the food, cleaning the gurdwara, or service to Sikhs and non-Sikhs outside the gurdwara.

Vahiguru Literally "Wow! God," but often translated as "wonderful Lord;" one of the names used for God, often used as a mantra and sometimes referred to as the gurmantra (God's mantra).

FURTHER INFORMATION

CALENDAR AND MAJOR FESTIVALS IN SIKHISM

The dates given below are according to the Nanakshahi calendar, which will be introduced from Vaisakhi 2003, subject to approval by the Shiromani Gurdwara Parbandhak Committee in Amritsar. In the Nanakashahi calendar, the Sikh year begins with Vaisakhi, which falls on 14 April. Celebrations that relate to events in the lives of the Gurus are called *gupurbs*.

14 April, Vaisakhi – introduction of the institution of the Khalsa by Guru Gobind Singh in 1699.

16 June – martyrdom of Guru Arjan.

16 August – installation of the Adi Granth, the first authorized collection of gurbani, by Guru Arjan in the newly built Harmandir Sahib (Golden Temple) in Amritsar.

20 October – installation by Guru Gobind Singh of the Guru Granth Sahib as his successor, ending the line of human Gurus.

21 October – martyrdom of Guru Gobind Singh, who died of his injuries after an assassination attempt.

25 October, Divali – Sikhs remember the return to Amritsar of Guru Hargobind from unjust imprisonment in the Gwalior fort. He delayed his release until he had secured the freedom of 52 Hindu princes, who had also been unjustly imprisoned.

8 November – Guru Nanak's birthday. Although the actual date is 14 April, the occasion is celebrated on 8 November to avoid two important Sikh events being celebrated on the same day.

24 November – martyrdom of Guru Tegh Bahadur, who died upholding the religious freedom of Hindus and Sikhs.

5 January – birthday of Guru Gobind Singh in Patna.

SIKH GROUPS

The Sikh Coalition
Promotes Sikh identity, rights with a legal center, women's program, youth program, and educational publications.
P.O. Box 7132
New York, N.Y.
10150–7132
Website: www.sikhcoalition.org

Sikh Study Circle
A non-profit religious body promoting Sikh identity and values, especially in Texas.
Irving Sikh Center
834 N. Nursery Road
Irving
TX 75061
Website: www.sikhstudy.com

WEBSITES

A variety of websites are moderated by members of the Sikh community. Many have links to other websites. Some of the best ones are listed below.

www.gurdwara.us
Sikh gurdwaras in the U.S. are listed alphabetically by state.

www.sikhnet.com
www.sikhs.org
Excellent sites and useful starting places, with links to numerous other websites.

www.allaboutsikhs.com
Particularly useful for the school age group.

www.sikhtoons.com
A recent website that is still developing; has a range of cartoons about different aspects of Sikhism.

www.sikhe.com
Free up-to-date information about Sikhs and Sikhism, including useful web links and a summary of newspaper reports from India, the U.K. and other parts of the Sikh Diaspora.

www.sikhcybermuseum.com
Another more recent site, allowing visits to a variety of places with exhibits relating to Sikhism and Sikh history.

www.sgss.org
Website of the Singh Sabha gurdwara in Hounslow, west London, which helps Sikhs and others locally, nationally, and internationally.

FURTHER READING

The Sikh Experience by Philip Emmett (Hodder and Stoughton, 2nd edition 2000).

Meeting Sikhs, Editor Joy Barrow (Christians Aware, 1998). Contains chapters by the leading scholars of Sikhism, and members of the Sikh community, in the U.K.

Teach Yourself Sikhism by W. Owen Cole (Hodder and Stoughton, 2nd edition 2003). Excellent reference book.

The Sikhs: Their Religious Beliefs and Practices by W. Owen Cole and Piara Singh Sambhi (Sussex Academic Press, 2nd edition 1995).

The Name of My Beloved: Verses of the Sikh Gurus, translated by Nikky-Guninder Kaur Singh (Harper Collins, 1996).

The Simple Guide to Sikhism by Sewa Singh Kalsi (Global Books, 1999).

INDEX

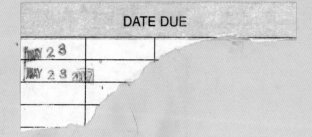